BOOK HOUSE

Author: **Jasminka Petrović** worked in marketing and journalism for many years before becoming a full-time writer. She is a regular contributor to two children's magazines and is the author of several books for young people.

Illustrator: **Dobrosav Živković** graduated from the Academy of Applied Arts at Belgrade University in 1985. Since then he has worked in advertising, marketing and children's magazines and has illustrated over 60 books.

Translated by Predrag Sibinović

Editor of this edition: Penny Clarke

Consultants: Dr Kristina Routh
            Jan Rees

© Kreativni centar 2000
© Book House MMII

Published in Great Britain in 2002 by
Book House, an imprint of
The Salariya Book Company Ltd
25 Marlborough Place
Brighton BN1 IUB

Falkirk Council	
LB	
Askews	
J306.7	£8.99

Visit The Salariya Book Company at:
www.salariya.com
www.book-house.co.uk

A catalogue record for this book is available from the British Library.

ISBN 1 904194 52 4

Printed and bounded by Publikum, Yugoslavia.

The SEX Files

by Jasminka Petrović
Illustrated by Dobrosav Živković

BOOK HOUSE

An introduction... (sort of)

Hello darlings!
I'm **Aunt Sybil**. I think sex is very important for every human being, especially teenagers. If you want to learn as many things as possible about sex and be sure they are accurate, stick to my advice.

Hello!
I'm **Aunt Gertie**. I agree that sex is very important for every one. If you want to make sure you don't do anything stupid, stick with me – I've been there too. We'll give you the information, but you're the one who'll know when it's right for you to use it.

It was impossible to learn about sex in our day. We made some awful mistakes. To find out if things are any better today we did some research. We discovered that people may have reached the moon, but on Earth things can still be pretty stone age. This book should get you to the era of the car, if not the moon rocket.

In our research we asked teens and pre-teens the following questions:

1. Are you interested in sex?
2. What is your first reaction when you hear the word sex?
3. Where do you get your information about sex?
4. Would you read a book about sex?

In answer to Question 1 '**Are you interested in sex?**', 98 out of 100 said they were '**very interested**' in sex. One said '**so, so**' and another '**not interested at all**'. The replies to Question 2 '**What is your first reaction when you hear the word sex?**', fell into two groups:

1. Excitement (Mark, aged 17)
2. Darkness (Kerry, 16)
3. Kylie (Steve, 15)
4. Kissing (Natasha, 13)
5. Getting Anna to go out with me (Sam, 16)
6. Love (Emma, 17)
7. Pamela Anderson (Dave, 18)
8. Screwing (Kevin, 16)
9. School trips (Katie, 17)
10. Condoms (Pete, 16)

1. My pet hamster (Sonja, aged 9)
2. Open your mouth and I'll tell you (Garry, 10)
3. Naked women (Jason, 11)
4. Sweeties (Holly, 10)
5. A joke Jason told me (Nick, 10)
6. None of your business (Jodie, 10)

8

*T*he answers to Question 3 '**Where do you get your information about sex?**', broke down into eight categories:

1. **Parents:** I tried asking my parents but they were embarrassed, so I stopped. What do parents know about sex, anyway?

2. **Teachers:** They're even more embarrassed than parents. Anyway, most look pretty sad, so they'll know even less about sex than parents.

3. **Friends:** What a load of rubbish – and it's all lies anyway.

4. **Medical books:** I tried reading them – wicked if you want to get to sleep.

5. **Pornography:** I read porn magazines until my father takes them (over).

6. **Sex education programmes:** I watch sex education programmes on children's TV. I know everything about how earthworms, bees and slugs do it.

7. **Porn movies:** I watch these whenever my parents go out for the evening – I wish they went out more often.

8. **The internet:** there are some good websites (see page 102), but remember there are phone bills to be paid!

The answer to Question 4 'Would you read a book about sex?', was 99 per cent 'YES'. Typical answers were 'can't wait', 'make sure there are pictures' and 'wouldn't you?' That 1 per cent? 'I want to play the guitar' was probably a joke, so we ignored it.

Besides answers to the questions the survey produced lots of comments. Many of them were based on myths. Some of the myths were around when we first started being interested in sex, so they've been around a long time! This book is written to dispel them.

Puberty or adolescence

This is the process during which a child becomes an adult. Puberty starts around the age of 11 and finishes at about 17. But these ages are averages. So if you start and/or end puberty earlier or later don't worry – you're quite normal.

Adolescence

Childhood

All kinds of changes take place during puberty: physical, mental, emotional, social and, of course, sexual. The cause of these changes are hormones in your body: oestrogen and progesterone if you're a girl and testosterone if you're a boy. They control the start of puberty, the growth of body hair, the development of breasts and penis, menstruation and the production of egg cells, the breaking of boys' voices and the production of sperm. Without these hormones you would not become an adult, but the process can be rough going – for you, your family and your friends.

Contents

BEFORE SEX

Am I normal?

Am I normal? This is probably the greatest cause of anxiety for anyone facing puberty or going through it.

Mood swings are among the first signs that you've started puberty. They're horrible. One moment you feel like you're still a child, and the next more grown up than your parents. It's those hormones – they'll make you feel bad-tempered, weepy, over the moon and every variation in between. You don't know who you are and, as your body begins to change, you may not like yourself that much. And if you don't

like you, who else will? The adults around you probably won't help much either. They'll find it as hard keeping up with your changing moods as you do. It may be the first time they've had to cope with a teenager since they were teens themselves all those years ago.

You'll feel confused and unsettled. You'll wonder if anyone will ever love you. You'll wonder what's the point of anything. You'll ask yourself (probably many times): 'Am I normal?' You are, absolutely, but don't take our word for it, do this test and find out for yourself.

Test your normality

Read each question carefully and think before answering it. Then make a note of your answer. Add up your Yes and No answers before looking at the conclusions. Cover them up if you think you might cheat and look at them first!

1. Do you look at yourself in a mirror whenever you get the chance? Yes/No
2. Do you daydream a lot? Yes/No
3. Do you hate school? Yes/No
4. Do you listen to loud music? Yes/No
5. Do you collect posters of pop stars, hunky film stars or pictures Yes/No
   of naked women? Yes/No
6. Do you quarrel with your family? Yes/No
7. Do you have frequent mood swings? Yes/No
8. Does everything bore you? Yes/No
9. Does everyone (especially those younger than you) bore you? Yes/No
10. Do you feel the need to do tests like this one? Yes/No

Conclusions:
If you answered YES to over half the questions YOU ARE NORMAL
If you answered NO to over half the questions YOU ARE NORMAL

Here's another test. It'll tell if you need to read the rest of this book. When you've done it count up the number of Yes answers and check the results below.

Wicked!

Are you adolescent?

1. Do you spend a lot of time locked in the bathroom?   Yes/No
2. Do you have acne?   Yes/No
3. Is hair growing on your body – not just your head?   Yes/No
4. If you're a girl, are your breasts growing?   Yes/No
   If you're a boy, is your penis growing?   Yes/No
5. If you're a girl, have your periods started?   Yes/No
   If you're a boy, is your voice deeper?   Yes/No
6. Do you think your arms are too long and your legs too short?   Yes/No
7. Do you fall in and out of love very often?   Yes/No
8. Does everyone else seem to have a better time than you?   Yes/No
9. No one understands you and no one loves you, right?   Yes/No
10. You think about sex a lot, but you're afraid to admit it, right?   Yes/No

| 9-10 Yes | 7-8 Yes | 5-6 Yes | 3-4 Yes | 0-2 Yes |

Aah!

Results:

9-10 Yes: Sure, you're adolescent, so read on.
7-8 Yes: You're facing adolescence, you need to read on.
5-6 Yes: You're clearly still an adolescent and need help, so read on – fast.
3-4 Yes: You're not there yet, but your parents might find this book helpful.
0-2 Yes: You know everything about everything, so write your own book – but as we've published this one please don't send it to us.

Some problems you and your friends may share

Parents. When you're with them you may wish you were a million miles away, though when you are you miss them. But parents do tend to...

ban everything you want to do:
- you can't go on that school trip!
- you'd better be in by ten!
- don't ever let me see you with that boy/girl with the nose/navel/tongue ring again!
- get off the phone!
- stop playing those video games!
- turn that awful music down!

order you to do things you hate:
- tidy your room!
- do your homework!
- get out of bed at once!
- apologise to your father!
- put on some clean socks!
- come and say hello to your aunt!

ask all the wrong questions:
- just who was at that party?
- you didn't join them in it did you?
- where have you been?
- who was that you were talking to?
- how was the maths test?
- did you do that?

Some parents just don't know when to stop!

Can't she see I'm grown up now!

Every day agony aunts like us get heaps of letters like this one:

'... it's difficult to get her to do her schoolwork, her marks are slipping. She hardly eats anything and is never at home. She spends all day with her friends. She won't tell me anything and she won't listen to me any more. She's got a boyfriend, but he's had problems and is quite a lot older than she is. I'm afraid he might trick her into having sex and I daren't even think about alcohol, drugs and AIDS. I'm beside myself with worry, I don't know what to do. I don't know what I did wrong...'

Aunt Gertie's ten tips – for this mum – and all parents and guardians:

1. Find out for yourself as much as possible about sex, contraception, AIDS and other STDs, alcohol and drugs.
2. Try to get your kids to talk about these subjects. Talk about them yourself.
3. Never ridicule them, their opinions or activities.
4. Help them face up to their emotions, dilemmas and fears.
5. Teach them to understand their sexual needs in an open, honest way.
6. Help them to learn self-respect.
7. Teach them to take responsibility for themselves and what they do.
8. Help them to recognise peer pressure, especially about drugs and sex.
9. Help them learn from their disappointments and failures.
10. Never forget – you are their most important role model.

You went through that stage too, so love your kids, trust them and help them become independent.

School

Love it or hate it, it's something we all have to go through. And it's very important where sex is concerned. You may (or may not) learn much about it in lessons, but school is great for love, intrigue and gossip. There are more opportunities for exchanging looks, notes, declarations, kisses and cuddles than most teachers have had school dinners. And the lavatory walls are an education in themselves.

Top tip:

Schools and school playgrounds may attract unpleasant characters. If you see anyone hanging around who clearly doesn't belong, tell a teacher at once.

Memo to anyone involved in sex education

Don't dodge this important subject. It may not be important to you any more, but it's an obsession with most of your class. And when you do talk about the subject, respect the kids by making it relevant and accurate. They'll respect you for doing this and they'll be much more likely to listen.

Aunt Gertie's five tips for teachers, school psychologists and sex educators:

> Don't forget – smile, relax and it'll be much easier to chat about sex with your kids.

1. Have as much up-to-date information as possible about sex, AIDS, alcohol and drugs.
2. Encourage the kids to get similar information – you can suggest reliable sources.
3. When you're going to discuss sex, love and personal relationships try to create a relaxed atmosphere in class, it'll make the discussion easier for everyone.
4. Organise lectures, debates and workshops about sex.
5. Your school will have a policy about sex education and informing parents. Follow it. You may even help to make the subject less embarrassing for them.

Arguments and rows

It's sad, but people have been having arguments and rows ever since there have been people. Bickering with your best friend, quarrelling with neighbours or war between states – rows take many forms. But it takes two people to have a row. One side always tries to provoke the other. Rows are usually caused by such unpleasant human characteristics as greed, selfishness, stupidity, anger, egocentricity, age differences and gender differences. Think of some recent rows you've had. What **really** caused them?

Arguments are part of adolescence – unfortunately. It's part of the process of growing up to become independent, self-reliant people. It's been the same throughout history. Ancient Greek authors (though they weren't ancient then) describe rows between parents and teenagers which sound just like rows between parents and teenagers today. The row is the same, it's just the scenery and clothes that have changed (and the language too).

Shyness and embarrassment

Shyness and embarrassment are the twin curses of adolescence. Everyone, male and female, suffers from them, some more, some less. They come in two forms: quiet and noisy. If yours is the quiet form, you'll look pale, feel tense and queasy, and be quite unable to think of anything to say. If yours is the noisy type, you'll look red in the face, feel rather light-headed, be overactive and much too talkative and you won't notice the hints to 'shut up, for goodness sake'. Several kids in our survey (see pages 8 and 9) commented that, **'I get even shyer when other people notice I'm shy'** and **'I am embarrassed because I'm changing constantly and don't know who I am'.**

It's easier said than done, but don't feel embarrassed, or even worse, guilty, because you're growing up. You are changing – so what? Every adult has done so too. Don't be scared of the changes, they'll bring new opportunities. And your parents will even start listening to your opinions – and that MUST be a change for the better!

Be patient! Don't be too hard on yourself. Accept your new face, your changing body and your new opinions. And try to accept the same changes you see in your friends. Making fun of them won't help – it's a childish response and you're growing up. Everyone goes through this stage and you're all, in your different ways, in it together. And adolescence does end!

Tips for tackling shyness:

1. Ignoring shyness isn't easy, but try thinking about something else – particularly something that's funny.
2. Willpower won't stop you blushing. But you'll stop more quickly if you can relax and ignore the blushes.
3. Talk to others about your shyness, ask how they deal with theirs. Don't pretend you don't suffer from it, but do remember your shyness doesn't bother other people as much as it bothers you.
4. Try to ignore teasing. Talk about something else.
5. Concentrate on the person you're talking to and what interests them. Thinking about them will take your mind off yourself and your shyness.

What about shyness in sex?

The closer you are to the person you love the less shy you'll be! Don't be negative! At the start of the relationship concentrate on what you like about yourself and not the things you dislike. And absolutely don't burden him/her with your complexes. As the relationship develops you'll both discover all sorts of new sides to your characters. That's (just) one of the great things about love.

> Oh dear, I wanted this to happen so much but now I feel shy about taking my clothes off, worried by my total inexperience and embarrassed when the light is on.

> Oh dear, I wanted this to happen so much but now I feel shy about taking my clothes off, worried by my total inexperience and embarrassed when the light is on.

Top tip:

Don't worry, these feelings are quite normal. Relax, mention them, enjoy the joke that you both feel the same, and the same about each other, and you'll soon forget them.

Mood swings

Mood swings, as we've already mentioned, are a nightmare – for you and everyone around you. One moment you could conquer the world and the next you're the most pathetic creature around. If they haven't hit you yet, they will – but, like adolescence, it's not a life sentence, it just feels like one!

One of the most unnerving things about mood swings is the speed with which they hit you. One moment everything is fine, you're popular, you've been asked to a party, lessons are going OK (well, you're getting reasonable grades), you haven't a spot in sight, and that great boy/girl you see on the way to school smiled at you this morning.

Then, bang. Something, anything, nothing, out of the blue hits you sideways. No one likes you, wants to know you. Your face is covered in spots (there's the tiniest of ones on your chin, it's been there for days and you hadn't given it a second's thought), your hair's lank and greasy (it's no different from when you got up this morning), you cut yourself shaving and that blonde who smiled at you yesterday must be laughing herself silly at the plaster you had to put on to stop the bleeding.

Hang on in there, your mood WILL change.

Mood swings reflect the complexities of our natures. Everyone's character is made up of a mixture of all the feelings you'll experience in extreme form during a mood swing.

Do they still teach the theory of pendulums in science? If they do, you'll know that pendulums swing backwards and forwards. So, when life seems awful, try to remember your personal pendulum will swing back up again. . .

. . . and things will change and the sun will come out again for you (even if it's actually pouring with rain). Once you're through adolescence you'll discover you're made up of all sorts of emotions and feelings. You may no longer feel you could conquer the world (that'll make life easier for you and everyone else), but you'll also realise that you're not the pathetic individual you sometimes felt like. It's quite a slog, but you'll make it!

Acne

The terror of all teenagers! All those hormones make the sebaceous glands in your skin go into overdrive. The result? Spots. Mostly on your face, chest and back, but always when you don't want them – like just before a new date.

Mum's advice: Don't touch your face with dirty hands!

Friend's comment: You can't see them at all!

Grandad's advice: Get your hair cut, your long greasy hair's the cause!

Beautician's advice: Wash your face with lukewarm water and mild soap once or twice a day.

Our advice: Outdoor exercise and don't look in a mirror for at least two years!

Medical advice: You'll grow out of it. But if it's really serious go to see your doctor.

Friend's comment: She's got them too!

Dad's advice: It's time you grew up!

Sister's advice: Put a paper bag over your head!

Grandma's advice: Eat more fruit and vegetables!

Don't worry, I had acne when I was your age, and is there any problem now?

Of course not, but when you were fifteen you thought you needed a skin graft!

Sex

It's everywhere and where would we be without it? There would be few films, fewer soap operas and almost no pop records! And, most importantly, no babies!

But we must make it absolutely clear that this book is **not** a guide to making love. It is a guide to help you increase your sexual knowledge. This means learning self-analysis, self-respect, decision making and understanding your body and sexuality. It also means knowing, understanding and tolerating others.

Sexuality is part of your personality. Everyone has sexual feelings, but we all express them differently. That is why it's so important to respect other people's sexuality.

Sex is natural and normal and everything we feel comfortable with or do with the consent of our partners is OK. If sex does not harm anyone it should not be condemned. We are all responsible for our own actions and their consequences.

Some possible differences between you and your friends

Ways of thinking – it's different between men and women and from one person to another.

Girls usually have thoughts like these:

How do I approach him?
Where will I go tonight?
What should I wear?
Why
 - aren't my breasts bigger?
 - isn't my waist smaller?
 - don't I have more money?
 - don't I have an older and smarter sister/friend?

Boys usually have thoughts like these:

How do I approach her?
Where will I go tonight?
Why
 - isn't my penis bigger?
 - isn't my nose smaller?
 - don't I have more money?
 - don't I have an older and smarter brother/friend?

Comment: Isn't it amazing how similar the thought processes are?!

Height

Your height depends mostly on your genes, though diet also plays a part. We can guarantee that perhaps before, definitely during and possibly after puberty, you'll be dissatisfied with your height and everything else about you. Don't worry – that's quite normal.

Body image

Among all the uncertainties of adolescence one thing is sure: at some point you'll hate the way you look. You'll feel too fat, too thin, too short, too tall, too dark, too fair etc, etc. It's no use us saying don't feel like this, because you won't take any notice. All the same, try not to – adolescence does end!

The tyranny of the scales

If you don't like yourself avoid this instrument of torture. If you do weigh yourself what you see will be something like this:

Too fat

Too tall

Too light

Too thin

Too short

Too heavy

Weight

Weight is part of body image but it's not the whole story. It's perfectly possible to be the same height and wear the same size clothes as your friend, but weigh more. Why? Think of how many bones there are in your body. If each one of yours weighs only a gram or two more than your friend's bones it's easy to see why you weigh more. It's the weigh (sorry – we couldn't resist the pun) you're made. It's quite natural and there's nothing you can do about it, so try to accept it.

However, what is not natural is when people are really, really fat. 'Obese' is the medical term. Sometimes there is a medical reason for their size. But more often it's too much junk food – sugary drinks, fat-laden hamburgers, pizzas and chips – and not enough exercise. If you have anyone like this in your group don't tease them. Being very overweight can cause serious health problems and they probably hate their body image too.

Do they still use that awful term 'puppy fat'? They did when I was your age. I hated it, but they were right, the fat did go. And now look at me...

... you've got middle-aged spread!

It's great to be different!

We've come a long way from the days when women were regarded as men's inferiors. We're all equal now! Or are we? If you're a girl does it matter if you can't, say, lift something as heavy as your boyfriend? And if you're the boyfriend it's really nothing to boast about because, size for size, men generally have more muscle than women.

But what's this got to do with sex?

It's got everything to do with sex. We know that appearance and sexuality are not the same, but we didn't when we were adolescents. So why should kids today? Don't you remember the hours we spent worrying over our appearance? My hair was too straight (OK it's permed now), yours was too curly. You hated your freckles. I cursed my glasses. You were so proud because your bust started developing before mine. Look at magazine adverts today, kids worry about the same things as we did. And it's probably worse for boys. Somehow people expect girls to worry about these things, but not boys. But why shouldn't boys worry? They're growing up too.

But I still don't see what it's got to do with sex?

It's obvious. The body and sex are very closely linked, especially at puberty. But once puberty's over, the minute obsession with your appearance will fade. Until then be patient – I know it's difficult but at least try!

Voice

His voice is every teenage boy's nightmare. One moment it's the voice he, and everyone else, knows well. The next second (we're not exaggerating) it's a man's deep voice. And what's worse, these changes are unpredictable and uncontrollable. The voice can change in the middle of a sentence. And it's so obvious to everyone around you. Every man has gone through this – that fact may not help much, but it's true.

Top tip:

Your voice will take a year or two to change completely. It will seem an eternity, but eternity is **much** longer!

Before

Body hair

Everyone has body hair. During adolescence it starts to grow in places it didn't grow before: in the armpits and the genital area. Hair also begins to grow on boys' faces, chests and backs.

After

Baldness only seriously affects men. The majority of bald men lose their hair later in life but occasionally baldness can occur in your teenage years.

More body hair

Facial hair consists of a moustache (hair on the top lip) and beard (hair on the chin and cheeks). Pubic hair grows in the genital area. It is not always the same colour or texture as the hair on the head. Many men find a woman's pubic hair very attractive.

Your body and facial hair have nothing to do with your overall attractiveness or what other people think of you. Any 'friend' who says otherwise isn't a friend.

But if you insist on seeing yourself as unattractive, with or without hair, you can't expect anyone else to think you're attractive.

Breast size

The source of enormous anxiety and much envy.

Breasts - four basic facts

1. Whatever their size you won't be satisfied with them.

2. Whatever their size your friends will tease you about them.

3. Whatever their size ALL your friends will have bigger ones.

4. Whatever their size, they'll look bigger if you walk tall with your shoulders back. Breasts are a wonderful addition to the body – unless you're a man that is.

We don't want to bore you, but your attractiveness does not depend on the size of your breasts.

If your loved one really loves you he will love your breasts, whatever their size. He will enjoy looking at them and caressing them, and you will enjoy being looked at and caressed.

Menstruation

Menstruation – also known as periods or time of the month – is bleeding from the uterus (see page 40) that occurs approximately once a month and lasts for between three days and a week. Obviously, only women menstruate. Menstruation begins in puberty and ends at the menopause.

What is menstruation?

Each month an egg is discharged from one of a woman's two ovaries. This is called ovulation ('ova' is Latin for 'egg') and occurs about half-way through the menstrual cycle. The egg goes down the Fallopian tube from the ovary to the uterus (or womb). If a woman has sex without any contraceptives at this time a sperm may join the egg in the Fallopian tube and fertilise it. This means the woman is pregnant (see page 74), the egg stays in the womb and her periods stop.

If the egg is not fertilised both the egg and the lining of the uterus are ejected as blood: menstruation. Then the cycle, which is controlled by hormones, begins again. The length of the cycle varies, but menstruation usually occurs every 28 to 32 days. Although your periods are likely to be erratic at first, they will settle into a regular cycle. You may get stomach cramps, back pain, mood swings, painful breasts, tiredness and irritability before and/or during your periods.

It will probably take a while for your periods to settle down into the regular cycle described above. It's horribly embarrassing to start bleeding if you have no protection with you. Avoid this worry by putting a tampon or sanitary towel into your school bag for emergency use. And if any woman tells you she's never had such an emergency – don't believe her!

If you miss a period talk to your mother, but if that's difficult talk to the school nurse, your teacher or your doctor.

Your first period will probably happen without any warning, though afterwards you may realise you felt slightly unwell (see opposite). But, equally, you may not. When your first period begins don't panic. Go to the nearest lavatory and put a sanitary towel, lavatory paper or paper towel in your pants. Then, if you're at school, go to the person who deals with such things as personal development – or whatever your school calls it. If you're at a friend's house do the same then tell her or her mother. Do the same if you're out and then go home as soon as you can. Once your periods have begun, keeping a note of the date each one starts will help you avoid unpleasant surprises. Don't forget that once your periods start you can get pregnant.

Missing a period doesn't automatically mean you're pregnant and if you haven't had sex with anyone you can't be. As we've said, your body is coping with so many changes that you may miss a period or two. But do tell someone – worrying on your own really does make things seem worse.

Sanitary towels and tampons soak up menstrual blood. Towels are used externally; tampons are inserted into the vagina. Both should be changed at least every four hours, more often if they're bloodsoaked. Don't leave a tampon in if it's not necessary because germs can build up and cause infection. Tampons and towels come in various sizes and thicknesses for light or heavy periods. Each has advantages and disadvantages. Try both and decide for yourself.

Tampon

Towel

You may not feel up to all your usual activities during a period. Sex isn't prohibited, or impossible, but is likely to be messy. It's up to you and your partner.

And don't believe the old story that you can't get pregnant if you're having your period – YOU CAN!

Sexual organs

The penis

At last – something about sex! I thought we'd never get to the point.

Women may have to suffer periods, but at least their sexual organ isn't visible. Look at yours. It's grown, but not like your friend's! His is bigger. It's probably thicker too. But if yours is smaller what makes you think that bigger is better? When you get over your shyness and talk seriously to your girlfriend, you'll probably be surprised at what she and her friends say on the subject.

Yours

Everyone else's

Sexual organs vary in size. Sometimes penises that are roughly the same size when limp become quite different when erect. And the same penis can vary in size depending on the erection. The size of your penis has nothing to do with your sexiness or virility.

Anything you look at from above looks smaller than it is. So change the view point! Try looking at your penis from the side in a mirror. It'll look a whole lot bigger. Not convinced? If you're still obsessed about size, draw up this table and start measuring – but getting a life is much more fun!

Table:

Date					
Exact time of measurement					
Pre-erection length					
Length during erection					
Post-erection length					

Apart from the size of your penis, you may worry that it is bent to the left or the right when it's erect. Very, very few men actually have dead straight penises. So, if a bent willy is bad for sex, how come there are so many couples about?

If it's any comfort (it won't be if you're that worried, but listen anyway) women's sexual organs vary in size too, so you're not alone.

The clitoris

An important part of a woman's sex organs is the clitoris. About the size of a pea, the clitoris is on the outside of the vagina. It's full of nerve endings and is a woman's main erogenous zone (see page 66).

The appearance of the sexual organs is not as important as their real purpose – giving each other pleasure.

Although both male and female sex organs have proper names, penis and vagina, they also have lots of nicknames. Many of them are used as swear words – and as I don't swear you probably know more of these words than I do!

Boys

At puberty you'll begin to have erections. In other words your penis will become erect and hard. When you have an orgasm, either through masturbation or sex with your partner, sperm cells will be in the fluid that you ejaculate.

Just below your penis is your scrotum which contains your two testicles, one a little lower than the other. Sperm is produced in the testicles.

Girls

The vagina is the flexible muscular passage about seven to ten centimetres long from a woman's uterus or womb. Menstrual blood and babies pass down it and the penis goes into it during sexual intercourse.

The vagina's opening on the outside of your body is protected by two pairs of lips – the labia.

The uterus, where babies develop before they pass down the vagina at birth, is also very muscular. It must be to accommodate the growing baby.

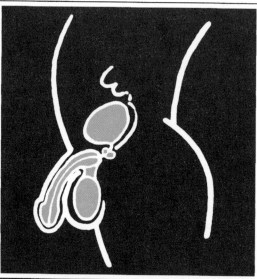

Do I really love him/her?

Flirting

Animal experts say that when primates like gorillas and chimpanzees fancy a member of the opposite sex they give him/her presents and find every excuse to touch him/her. The males swagger and the females simper. Sounds familiar? Well, humans are also primates.

Flirting may be the start of something serious, or just frivolous fun. Treat it lightheartedly until you're sure about the person who's flirting with you. Insecure or jealous people often think flirting equals sexual relations and see it as a threat. If your friend or partner reacts in this way, it's a pity, but you've learnt something useful about him/her. If your flirting wasn't just innocent fun, he/she has learnt something about you!

Infatuation

If one of your friends suddenly starts behaving oddly – doesn't listen, spends even longer on the phone than usual (and not to you), daydreams, isn't interested in all the usual things, talks endlessly about someone (not you) – you'll know he/she is suffering from infatuation. This very intense form of affection is usually one-sided and embarrassing for the object of the infatuation. But it's hard to love someone who doesn't respond, so infatuation soon fades.

Dear Diary

I am so happy I cannot find words to describe it. I saw HIM today. And I think he saw me. He was talking to his friend with the motorbike. He looked so cool. He was wearing trainers and a denim jacket and I LOVE him. I was at the bus stop with Kelly. She wanted me to go and speak to him. I didn't have the guts – anyway the bus might have come and I'd have missed it, then Mum'd have been cross. I almost did, but then the bus did come. He smiled and I think it was at me. Perhaps he'll be there tomorrow. I can't wait.

Yours,
Lauren

A few days later...

Dear Diary

Gloom. Gloom. Life is awful.
He was there again, but he
was talking to Sharon that
awful girl from the next
street, the one who always
hangs around with the boys.
They say she's done it
already – what a tart!

But Kelly's asked me to a
party on Saturday – perhaps
I'll meet someone there.

Yours,
Lauren

Love is...

Loving families, loving friends, falling in love.... Some people think love just means romantic emotions. Others identify love with sexual desire and attraction. Some say sexual relations should never take place without love, while others say that it is only through sexual relations that we can discover our real feelings about our partner.

There's a lot to be said for each of these views – there isn't a right or a wrong one, life would be easier if there was! But what is wrong is to force someone to do something they don't want to. Anyone who tells you that the only way to prove you love him/her is to have sex together when you don't want to is only proving that he/she doesn't love you and just wants to take advantage of you.

Many people try to solve the problem of loneliness by forming sexual relations, even if they aren't in love with the other person. But this doesn't solve anything – it usually just makes matters worse. You won't be able to fool yourself for long and then you'll feel cross and angry with yourself. And what use is that?

Being in love is a wonderful, amazing feeling whatever your age. But it has its ups and downs, as you'll discover. It's all part of growing up.

Breaking up

Breaking up marks the end of a relationship. Some people see breaking up as a great tragedy, others as a bit of a joke (if your partner comes into the second category you're better off without him/her). You'll know if a break up is on the horizon (for you or your friends) because you and your partner will start arguing (much) more than usual.

On a piece of paper, note down your answers to the questions below to see if the end is nigh for your relationship.

Are you breaking up?

1. You can't stand the sight of him/her.   Yes/No
2. You feel like throwing up when near him/her.   Yes/No
3. The thought of kissing him/her makes you gag.   Yes/No
4. You no longer ask him/her to go to parties with you.   Yes/No
5. You always avoid him/her.   Yes/No
6. You rubbish him/her whenever you can.   Yes/No
7. When he/she talks to you, you ignore him/her.   Yes/No
8. You refuse to enter lifts with him/her.   Yes/No
9. You wish his/her family would move.   Yes/No
10. You can't wait to get a new partner.   Yes/No

Five or more Nos? You're just about to break up.

Five Yes answers and five Nos? The break up has begun.

More than five Yes answers? You've already broken up. He/she just hasn't realised it!

Jealousy

Jealousy is an emotion like love. But love is positive, while jealousy is totally negative. To love someone is to trust them. Jealous people can't do this. Instead they try to keep 'their property' to themselves. Jealous people are actually very insecure, but don't feel sorry for them – just don't get involved with them.

A jealous man never lets his girlfriend out of his sight. He doesn't like parties – after all someone might 'steal' her. So they don't go out much. Instead they stay in, watching TV and videos, making love and bickering – especially bickering, because it's no fun being with a jealous man. If his girlfriend tries to leave, he may become emotionally unstable.

Note: Reread the above changing 'man' to 'woman', 'he' to 'she' etc, because jealous women behave in exactly the same way.

If you have a jealous partner, you may get to feel like this!

Jealousy is usually a sign the jealous person is insecure and disappointed with him/herself. It has nothing to do with love. In fact it can usually be guaranteed to destroy love.

I used to suffer from jealousy, but I cured myself. First I stopped comparing myself with other people. Then I tried to be as good as possible at everything I did. Starting was hard, but it got easier and it worked. If Fido could talk, he'd tell you what a sweet, unjealous person I am.

Fido

The telephone

If your parents think you spend too long on the phone, that's the best possible reason for having a mobile. It immediately improves relations with them, until the bills roll in, of course!

The advantages of calling your loved one by phone

1. He/she can't see your awkwardness, blushes, despair at rejection, anger during rows, tears when you break up.

2. It's often easier to say such things as:
   I love you.
   Will you go out with me?
   I want to make love to you.
   I've had enough of you.

The disadvantages of calling your loved one by phone

1. You can't take advantage of four of your senses, you can't see, smell, taste or touch each other.

2. The only sex acts possible over the phone are foreplay and playing with yourself (see page 50), but who knows what science may come up with!

The telephone is a great invention, but seeing your friends is much more fun. Being out with friends also means you're out of earshot when your parents grumble because you've been on the phone too long/not done your schoolwork/not tidied your room/not helped with the washing up.*

* Delete as appropriate

Computers and sex

Think of any subject today and computers are bound to be involved – sex is no exception, especially now there's e-mail and the internet. Why bother to handwrite love letters when you can do it on the computer **and** have your spelling checked!

E-mailing friends is fun. Chatting to people on the other side of the world is great. But are the people you're 'talking' to really who they say they are? How do you know? Some adults have used internet chatrooms to 'befriend' or 'groom' children and later met and harmed them. Sad, but true.

Pornography (page 91) is available on the internet. It can be frightening and shocking, and much of it is illegal. Via a computer screen seems a sad way to enjoy sex, but it has one advantage over the real thing – computer viruses cannot harm your health like real viruses.

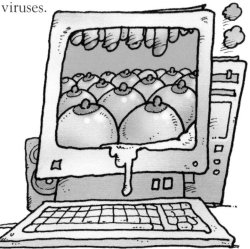

I don't want to interfere or spoil your fun, but if you agree to meet someone you've 'met' on the internet, please be careful. Meet in a public place, such as a café, and always tell someone where you're going first. Take some friends along. Tell the person you're going to meet that this is what you're going to do and if they show any sign of arguing or trying to persuade you to do something else, tell them that the meeting is off – forever.

And if anyone sends you anything indecent, or in any way unpleasant via e-mail, do tell your parents if possible, or, if you really can't talk to them about such things, tell a teacher.

I know you'll think I sound just like your parents, but don't skip this little paragraph. Exploring sex on the internet may make you feel very adult, especially if you can brag about it to friends who think they have better things to do with their time. You may think they are sad. But it's you who are sad. Why? Well, meeting people on the screen is a way of avoiding meeting people in real life. If you're too busy with fantasy friends, your real ones will stop asking you out. Eventually you'll have no friends and be a great example of a sad person. Is that your ambition?

Pornography and erotic literature have probably been around for as long as people have been able to read and write. Why? Sex has been around even longer!

Sexual Fantasies

Sexual fantasies are fun and harmless, especially good for whiling away the journey to school, on the beach or in bed. Naked bodies are generally a feature. But sexual fantasies are just that – fantastic and fun. Don't get so carried away by them that anything else is a disappointment. Fantasies mean you can be anyone you want and do whatever you want with whomever you want – but only in your imagination!

Top tip:
Avoid having fantasies in class – the lesson may be awful, but there's an essay to write afterwards and you need something to put in it.

Top tip:
Sharing fantasies is fun, but take care who you share them with, there are people (parents?) you might prefer not to know about them.

Masturbation

Masturbation, also known as playing with yourself, is enjoying sexual pleasure without the involvement of anyone else. As the phrase suggests, it means satisfying your desire by doing it to yourself.

All research shows that men are much more likely to masturbate than women. It's not because men are sex-obsessed and women aren't. It's because the penis is very accessible. Every time a boy urinates he touches his penis, so masturbation is a very small step. Most girls, however, only begin to masturbate in late adolescence.

Masturbation and sexual fantasies go together like, well, chickens and eggs. Boys usually find visual objects most stimulating, while girls generally prefer written descriptions. Perhaps that's why men reach orgasm faster than women – it's quicker to look at a picture than read a book!

If you don't really like masturbating, don't worry, there's NOTHING wrong with you!

It's none of your business, but there's **nothing** wrong with me!

You'd be surprised how common masturbating is. But it's not something most people talk about. Not only is it done in private, it's also frowned upon.

You'll go blind!

You'll go mad!

You'll die!

You'll make it shrivel!

It'll fall off!

You'll grow hair on your palms, and then everyone'll know!

You're wasting your sperm, you won't be able to have children!

An awful warning or a load of old rubbish?

*You'd be amazed the lengths people who disapprove of masturbation will go to try to put you off. They say all sorts of dreadful things will happen to your appearance so no one will ever, **ever** love you. If they were right, the human race'd have died out long ago!*

Don't EVER fall for stories about what masturbation will do to you! It has absolutely NO effect on your appearance. Is that clear?!

Parents and religions, among others, have condemned masturbation for thousands of years. They say it's 'unnatural'. It's only unnatural because sex is basically about having babies and ensuring the species continues. For that you do need two people. But masturbation is harmless and far better than having sex with someone who doesn't want to. And you can't get pregnant or catch sexually transmitted diseases (see page 83) by masturbating. And if you hear anyone using the old term 'self-abuse', it says more about them than it does about you.

Wet dreams

Wet dreams, also known as nocturnal emissions, happen to males when they're asleep both during and after puberty.

Sweet (wet) dreams?

There was once a young boy who tried to expel his sperm. Try as he might, he couldn't. He summoned a dream to help him. That didn't help. The dream summoned an erection. But still he had no luck. Exasperated, the erection summoned an orgasm. Success at last – the sperm was ejaculated.

Wet dreams, pluses: Everything is wonderful, you're the handsome hero and as for the heroine...!
Wet dreams, minuses: When it's over your bed is wet and your pyjamas are all sticky!

Hanging out

Hanging out with other people is very important for sexual relations – it's usually where they start! Hanging out with friends means you meet other people, go on dates, get closer to others, fall in love, hold hands, kiss, yawn, quarrel and make up, cheat on each other and sometimes even talk!

Dates can be classified as follows:

Order:
   The first; the last; the first, the last and never again
Numbers involved:
   Solo; twosomes (intimate); groups (herds)
Reaction:
   Extremely boring; boring; interesting; a blast

Dates

You'll always remember your first date. You'll probably still think about it occasionally when you're as old as your parents. What about asking them about their first one!

Try not to expect too much of your first date. Easier said than done! But if you don't and it doesn't work out too well you'll be less disappointed. It just could be the start of a blazing passion, better that than a blazing row – you know that old saying about playing with fire!

Go out whenever you have the time. 'I've nothing to wear', 'My hair needs washing', 'I've got a spot', 'I've got my period', 'I've no money' – excuses, excuses. The more you go out the more people you'll meet, and the more people you meet the greater your chance of making a good relationship.

You want your date just to be between you and the person you're dating. So did we, so did your parents. But until you really know each other, going out in a group is better. It's more fun, less hassle and also safer. Before you go out, tell someone in your family. Your parents are best – if you don't tell them they'll think you're hiding something. Say where you're going and roughly when you'll be back. You may think they're being nosy but they just want to know you'll be safe.

Kisses

You'll have had some already: from your family and the people who care about you. You'll have given some already: to your family, best friend (if you're a girl). You'll also have been expected to kiss family, relatives etc, etc. But we're not discussing those kisses. The kisses we **are** discussing are the ones we give our partners.

There are several different approaches to kissing, mostly depending on the age of those doing (or trying to do) the kissing.

Before puberty

I love you.

I think you're wonderful.

Do you love me?

This approach (see above) is foolish. It rarely works. When puberty starts you'll discover that kissing your friend is much better than kissing the notes you send them.

Puberty

At puberty you're older and more mature, so you approach things differently.

Question:
Have you ever kissed anyone like they do in films, tongue and all?

Answers:
Lots of times.
I stopped counting after the 100th time.
Not yet, but I can't wait.
Why ask – you know the answer.
'Course not, I don't want to catch anything.
None of your business.
Ask Kylie in form 7B.
Yes!
What do you think?

Question:
What do you feel when French kissing?

Answers:
My tongue feels tingly.
A hard-on.
Don't know yet.
You'll describe it better than me.
Nothing.
Indescribable.
I get hot.
If only you knew.

Top tip:

To enjoy kissing each other you should both keep good oral hygiene. Yes, that does mean cleaning your teeth at least twice a day and going to the dentist at least twice a year, but it's all in a good cause. And don't even think about smoking – kissing a smoker is like licking an ashtray.

Caressing and making out

Caressing and making out, together with kissing, represent foreplay (see page 60). While you kiss with lips and tongue, you caress with hands and fingers. Some people prefer kissing, some touching and stroking, others prefer a combination of the two. Try them all, there's no right or wrong. Just don't force things.

Hand on hand   OR   *Hand on knee*

Hand on shoulder   *Hand on thigh*

Hand on breast   *Hand on 'thing'*

Remember caressing only makes sense if you both enjoy it. If you don't, talk to each other to find out what is stopping the enjoyment. **Don't** row about it, that'll ruin everything.

Being relaxed

The more relaxed you both are the better the result. But 'result' doesn't just mean sexual intercourse and orgasm, it includes mutual closeness, tenderness and joy. If any one of these is missing the sex may be good at first, but the relationship will not, in the end, be a happy and lasting one.

Sometimes making out needs a special atmosphere, a dimly lighted (or quite dark) room (you may not feel shy, but he/she may), soft music and, of course, a partner. Sometimes just the partner is enough.

Top tip:

Areas to touch:
Your girlfriend's breasts and genitals

Areas not to touch:
Breasts and genitals of someone else's girlfriend

Now let us end this chapter and start the one you really want to read: Sex.

At last!

Going all the way

Petting

Petting includes everything mentioned so far – kissing, caressing, touching, masturbation. It doesn't include what this section covers – sexual intercourse, pregnancy and sexually transmitted diseases, such as AIDS.

In the past sex before marriage was forbidden. But couples still wanted sex. To let off their sexual tension, they turned to petting or mutual masturbation – you could call it a sort of external intercourse. Attitudes change, but petting's still popular!

Petting still has a great deal going for it. If you are a virgin, or have a new partner, it lets you both be intimate without having full sex. So it reduces the risk of pregnancy and sexually transmitted diseases almost to zero. Why 'almost'? Because there is NO such thing in life as 100 per cent certainty – except death, but that's another matter.

Before you start petting ask yourselves:
  What do I expect?
  Where are the boundaries?
  What happens next?

Sex, but only if you **both** want it.

Foreplay

Foreplay is the warm up period before sex begins.

Foreplay can last as long or as short a time as both of you want. If it's the first time you've had sex, or the first time with a new partner, and especially if you're both feeling shy and awkward, it's probably best to take things slowly and gently.

Foreplay can take different forms: a meal for two, a romantic walk, a loving phone call. Holding hands (though not if you're talking to each other on the phone), endearments and smiles help create the right atmosphere. Touching, caressing, passionate embraces and kisses will make you both more relaxed, and gentle teasing can help arouse sexual feelings. And taking each other's clothes off can be a wonderful pleasure.

Foreplay is especially important for the woman. Take time over it, even if you've made love together many times. She's not being difficult, she hasn't stopped loving you, but it usually takes a while for all the powerful muscles in her womb, that may one day support a baby, to relax. By taking time, not only do you show her you care, but it'll be much more enjoyable for you both – and isn't that what you both want?

Don't forget that in foreplay anything goes as long as you are both happy to do it.

Sexual intercourse

Making love, humping, screwing, banging and bonking are just some of the names for sexual intercourse – as you probably know anyway. And that's just the point we've got to....

Sexual intercourse begins the moment the penis (the male sex organ) penetrates the vagina (the female sex organ). For that to happen the male must have an erection – his penis becomes harder and bigger than usual. The sexual organs are in contact with each other and body movements become faster, which increases sexual excitement until the moment of orgasm (see page 67). Immediately after this the penis becomes soft again and intercourse is over. If and when the cycle is repeated depends on external factors (I must go to work/school/ the shops) and the sexual needs and capacities of the partners.

And don't forget that in sexual intercourse anything goes as long as you are both happy to do it.

Worried about having sex?

S ex is not a 'performance', although at first you'll probably both worry that you're not 'doing it right'. Instead of worrying, think of other things you do, like playing a musical instrument or in a sports team. You're probably much better now than when you started – so why should a sexual relationship be different?

But when you do begin to have sex with your partner try to find somewhere safe and private – snatched encounters and fears of being 'caught in the act' do nothing for anyone's sex life.

> You'll see all sorts of sexual scenarios on televison and in films. They always involve a handsome hero, a beautiful heroine and magnificent orgasms. I hope you don't need me to tell you that real life's not like that! So don't worry if you're not handsome/beautiful and your orgasms aren't earth-shattering – at least they're real!

B oys, are you worried that you don't know exactly where to put your penis? Unlike you, women have a special opening, the urethra, through which they pass urine. This is quite separate from the vagina – where you put your penis during intercourse. But don't worry, your penis is much too big to go into the urethra.

Everyone talks about a penis being 'hard', so won't it hurt me when it goes in?

W ell there's hard and hard. An erect penis is only hard by comparison with what it's like when it isn't! 'Stiff' would really be a better word. That's also why men are said to get 'erections' – their penis becomes stiff and stands out from their body. Amazingly, this stiffness is caused by blood. There are no bones in the penis, just lots of blood vessels which fill with blood when a man is aroused.

The muscles around the entrance to the vagina will probably be pretty tight at first, that's why foreplay (see page 60) is important to help you both relax. Putting a vaginal lubricant (you'll find them in any chemist) on your partner's penis – and him putting some on the lips around the entrance to your vagina – will also help make it easier for him to come into you.

What if my partner doesn't have an orgasm, am I doing it wrong? Am I a failure?

The short answer to the first question is 'not necessarily', and to the second is 'absolutely not'. Unlike men, women can thoroughly enjoy sex, yet not have an orgasm. It's the way they're made. Try not to worry about it (you will). Instead talk to her about it. You may find that she is feeling a failure because she hasn't had one and she may feel she is letting you down. The best way for you both to enjoy an orgasm, after you've talked to each other, is to relax and stop worrying.

There are easier ways to enjoy sex!

How you feel about your sexuality is likely to be influenced by the way you were brought up and the attitudes of the adults around you. Attitudes to sex are generally more relaxed now than they were even when your parents were teenagers. Try to respect their opinions, even if you feel they are very negative – you don't have to share them.

Don't let anyone make you think sex is wrong or something to be ashamed of, although becoming pregnant or catching an STD because you couldn't be bothered to use contraceptives certainly is.

People have sex for lots of reasons, among them curiosity, boredom, loneliness, revenge, fun, gain, 'everyone else is' and 'I'll be left out/laughed at if I don't'. But there is only one really good reason: love.

Sexual relations can be:

heterosexual – between people of different sexes
homosexual – between people of the same sex (see pages 72 and 73), or
bisexual – with people of either sex (see page 73).

Unprotected sex can result in sexually transmitted disease (STD) and/or pregnancy. And pregnancy means a baby. During sexual intercouse, the male orgasm causes a huge number of sperm to enter the uterus. If it is the right time in the menstrual cycle a sperm may fertilise an egg. This is the start of a pregnancy. Unless you can look after and support a baby until it grows up, getting pregnant is not clever.

All this talk – let's have some facts.

You're so impatient! A sperm can fertilise an egg for up to 48 hours after it has left the man's body. Egg cells are fertile for three to four days. If fertilisation doesn't take place the sperms die and are expelled from the woman's body. Unfertilised eggs also die and are expelled during menstruation. Using contraceptives (see page 78) will stop you (or your partner) becoming pregnant.

Phew, you do go on. It's a wonder anyone gets round to sex!

Say YES, say NO

It's easy to get into a sexual relationship, especially if you haven't had many, without knowing why you are doing so. Some people cannot express their feelings for their partners in words. Others long for tenderness. Others fear they may be dumped if they won't go to bed with someone. A (very) few yearn for sex but always say no. Though you might think that saying yes to sex just involves your body, there's more to it than that. Saying yes to sex involves mental, emotional, social and ethical considerations. That's why you must say what you mean. Saying YES and meaning NO, or vice versa, is unfair and confusing – to you both.

GIRLS – Learning to say NO when you mean NO is as important as learning to put make-up on properly. NO is especially important on a first date. However bright the moonlight and however irresistible he might seem, get to know him better before having sex.

BOYS – Saying NO is important if you don't want a reputation as someone who chases every female in sight. You might find one you really like, but with that sort of reputation, why should she believe you feel differently about her?

Erogenous zones

These are parts of your body that have masses of nerve endings. The main erogenous zones are: the mouth, breasts (especially the nipples), the nape of the neck, the inner and upper thighs and, of course, the genitals. If you haven't already, you'll soon find these zones because caressing them gives particular pleasure. There are other, lesser, erogenous zones, but you can discover those for yourself!

Mutual exploration of erogenous zones is fun – and an excellent way of strengthening the bond between you. You'll also find that different people enjoy different erogenous zones. What gave the greatest pleasure to one partner may not do so to a new one. But a new partner can also reveal new pleasures.

Top tip:

It isn't just what you touch that matters. How you touch matters just as much. Some people respond to gentleness, others to firmness. Everything is fine as long as you both agree to, and enjoy, it.

Orgasm

Orgasm, also known as coming or the climax, is the shortest, but most exciting, part of sex. It is accompanied by a feeling of warmth, harder breathing, faster heartbeat, muscle spasms, contraction of the uterus (in women), ejaculation of sperm (in men), and perhaps also by sighs, moans, groans and creaking (of the bed). Afterwards the entire body feels relaxed and satisfied. However, the downside of orgasm is an unwanted pregnancy. And it's the male orgasm, or ejaculation, that's decisive here – a woman can become pregnant even if she doesn't have an orgasm.

Don't worry if you and your partner don't have orgasms at the same time. Simultaneous orgasms are mostly found in movies and soap operas. In contrast, problems with erections only occur in real life!

Despite what our grandmothers told us, women do have orgasms. However, it's perfectly possible (and normal) for a woman to enjoy sex without having one.

Top tip:

Relax, play with each other, have your contraception ready, make love and enjoy yourselves! And if you don't have an orgasm? It's not the end of the world. It won't be the first (or last) time this happens – to you or anyone else.

Virginity

Once regarded as a girl's greatest asset and protected by ever-vigilant adults, today it's less highly rated. Even so, the thought of the 'first time' may cause anxiety and concern that it will be painful (see page 62).

Most girls have a thin tissue of skin, the hymen, stretched across the entrance to their vagina. When the penis enters the vagina during a girl's first sexual experience it must go through the hymen. This can cause a stab of pain and bleeding. The pain doesn't last and you can put a folded towel under you to absorb any blood. If there is neither pain nor blood that's great – your hymen probably tore quite naturally while you were doing sports. Very rarely the hymen does not grow at all, that too means no pain or bleeding.

The best sex comes when you really love someone and have been around long enough to know that you do. It also helps to have an empty flat, a candle-lit dinner for two, soft music, warmth (not necessary in summer!), a comfortable bed and the one you love. And most of you haven't got any of these things yet.

VIRGIN
Everyone except me has done it!

What's the rush?

VIRGIN
I don't want to miss the Simpsons!

Please don't rush into things. Just because 'everyone' else says they're doing it doesn't mean they are. You'll always remember your 'first time'. Do you really want to remember it as something you'd rather forget?
And remember, if anyone says you can't get pregnant during your 'first time' they're talking **absolute rubbish** – and dangerous rubbish at that!

I AM AFRAID OF
  pain
  pregnancy
  farting accidentally
  my mother coming in
  making a fool of myself
  not knowing what to do
  not feeling anything at all
  not being able to get a hard-on
  what will happen afterwards
  rumours about us
  him/her using me...

Are any of your fears in this list? Does knowing that others have fears make it easier? Or worse because your fears were different?

Occasionally the 'first time' gets postponed more than once. This can happen if the two partners are shy and possibly inexperienced. As long as both partners want the postponement equally, there's nothing wrong. But you need to be sure that one of you isn't just teasing, and really should have said 'No' to start with.

Warning all females

Don't expect too much from your first sexual experience, because you aren't very likely to get much, especially if it's his first time too. Your feelings will be so strong, you'll both find it difficult to relax. Yes, of course you want to find out what an orgasm's like. Who knows, you might just be one of the lucky ones – miracles can happen.

Warning all males

Don't expect too much from your first sexual experience, because you aren't very likely to get much, especially if it's her first time too. Expect problems with your erection, getting your penis into her vagina which is likely to be quite tight, premature ejaculation.... Don't expect fiery sex and an earthquake of an orgasm. But don't worry, all this is quite normal. You have nothing to worry about!

Positions

There are all sorts of positions in which you can make love, some more possible than others. These are some of the best known:

1. Him on top
2. Her on top
3. Sitting down
4. From behind
5. Kneeling
6. Him standing
7. He wants to…
… she won't

Positions for advanced acrobats (or the desperate)

1. Male fantasy

2. Female fantasy

3. Mutual fantasy

4. What's she trying to tell me?

5. What's he trying to tell me?

6. He's fallen asleep

7. She wants to…

…he won't

Top tip:

Leave some of the more extreme positions until you have mastered the basics. Great sex doesn't need great acrobatic or athletic skills – if it did most of us would have real problems!

Oral sex

This involves stimulating the genitals with your tongue and mouth. You can do it to each other in turn or at the same time – that's what '69' means. Some love oral sex, others hate it. Some are scandalised (have they tried it?), some amazed, some indifferent. What's your position (that's a pun, but, yes, a very bad one)? Whatever you think, remember: you must both enjoy whatever you do together. Forcing someone to do something they don't want to do is the best recipe for bad sex there is.

Anal sex

Sticking to the traditional entrances and exits is so much easier! But to stop you nagging, here goes....

The skin around the anus, or rectum, has masses of nerve endings. Stimulating it can be pleasant for both men and women. Using a condom is a must for this type of sex because of all the germs inside the anus and the possibility of getting the HIV virus. But because the anus was not intended for penetration anal sex can be very painful and cause bleeding. So now you know...!

Homosexuality

Homosexual men are those who have sexual relations with other men. In many Western countries homosexual men live openly with each other and in some they can marry. Homosexuals in long-established relationships may even adopt children. Some people view homosexuality with understanding, others with horror, while others just don't want to know. Whatever you, or anyone else, may think, there have always been and always will be homosexuals. No one knows why some men are sexually aroused by men and not women. It's just the way they are. During puberty boys often show off their penises, compare their size and even masturbate together. This is natural curiosity and competitiveness, not homosexuality.

Lesbians

Lesbians are homosexual women. In other words, they too fall in love with members of their own sex, have sexual relations with them and might live together. The same things that go for homosexual men also go for lesbians.

During puberty girls are usually very kind and caring to one another, spending a lot of time together and often holding hands and walking arm in arm. These are signs of friendship, closeness and allegiance rather than lesbianism.

Bisexuality

A surprising number of people are bisexual, which means they can enjoy sex with both their own and the opposite sex. However, the majority of people find it most enjoyable with members of the opposite sex.

Someone with a good sex life

One of the best things about sex

Relaxation – good sex reduces tension and gives a wonderful feeling of relaxation and satisfaction.

If you want a really good sex life, you need to know exactly what you want of yourself and your partner. This is not so simple, especially during adolescence with all the mood swings we've already discussed. Before starting a sexual relationship try asking yourself questions like those on the right. By taking responsibility for yourself and your actions, you'll feel stronger, more secure and happier. Don't believe me? Give it a try – it doesn't cost anything!

Questions to ask myself:

Am I ready?
Who do I want to have a sexual relationship with?
Why do I want it?
Why him/her?
Where will we make love?
Am I in love?
What do I expect?
What are the consequences?
What contraception will I/we use?

Pregnancy

Pregnancy is the most obvious result of sex if you haven't used contraception. You may have heard that you (or your partner) is not fertile (cannot get pregnant) all the time. This is true. You may also have heard that you (or she) is only fertile on the 14th, 15th and 16th days of your/her monthly cycle. This is NOT true. Few women have absolutely regular monthly cycles and no teenager ever has. If you've been stupid enough to have sex without using contraception and you/she isn't pregnant, you're ***** lucky and don't count on getting away with it again.

Pregnancy lasts nine months. It involves discomfort, visits to the doctor, expense – and that's before the baby's born. So what's all that going to do for your futures? And don't forget the future of the new person either.

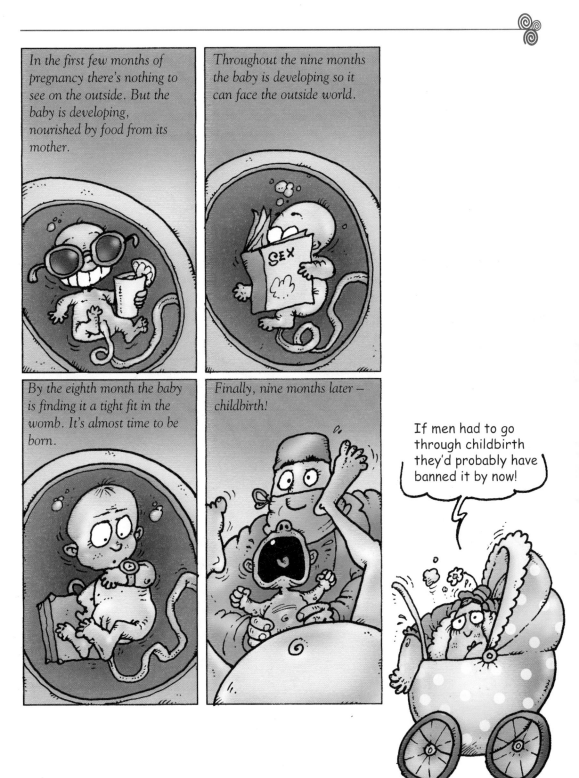

In the first few months of pregnancy there's nothing to see on the outside. But the baby is developing, nourished by food from its mother.

Throughout the nine months the baby is developing so it can face the outside world.

By the eighth month the baby is finding it a tight fit in the womb. It's almost time to be born.

Finally, nine months later — childbirth!

If men had to go through childbirth they'd probably have banned it by now!

Basically sex is about procreation – having babies. Without babies no species could go on existing. Scientists say dinosaurs died out because a massive meteorite hit the earth. What do they know? Could be the females just had bad headaches and aspirin hadn't been invented!

The best thing for any baby is to be born into a loving family, a family which wants it. The worst thing for a baby is to be born because its parents, especially if they're still going through adolescence, didn't bother to use contraception. That's a disaster all round.

Expert advice

As you go through adolescence you'll discover you're surrounded by experts: experts on sex (don't do it – wait till you're grown up), experts on adolescents (we never did that when I was your age), experts on social change (what a state the world is in, things were **much** better when I was young). You name it, there'll be an expert on it.

You'll soon notice that almost all the 'advice' will be negative and all the 'experts' will be as old as your parents, if not older. Don't worry – it's quite normal. The older generation is having to come to terms with you changing – perhaps you aren't quite as cute as you were and have you **really** never answered back?

The older generation has complained about the younger one ever since there were two generations, and you wait – you'll be doing it too, when you're part of the older generation!

Hygiene

Hygiene is important. It may involve doing things you've not been too keen on doing before: showering, cleaning your teeth regularly, washing your hair before it's a lank mess, getting it cut and so on. It may also mean not doing things – like not picking your nose, or at least not in public.

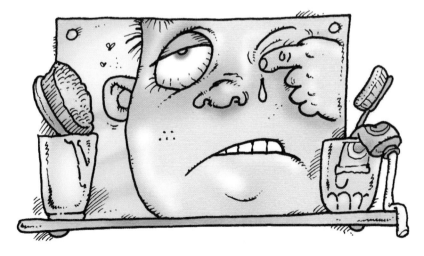

No one enjoys having sex with a partner whose cleanliness is poor. Bathing or showering together is a good way of avoiding this problem. It's also a good place for foreplay.

If your partner is reluctant to have sex, perhaps he/she is worried about becoming pregnant or getting a sexually transmitted disease. The next section tells you what you need to know. And if you read it together you'll both know!

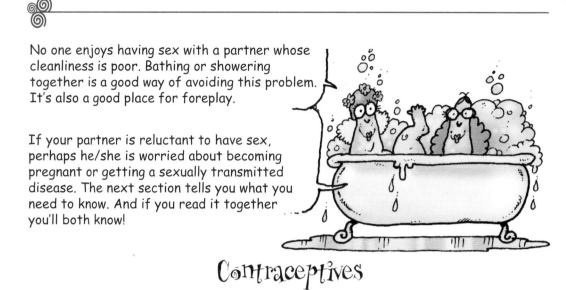

Contraceptives

Contraceptives prevent pregnancy. Correction:contraceptives used properly prevent pregnancy. Like anything else, if you don't follow the instructions they don't work. And never forget, or let anyone persuade you otherwise, there is no 'safe' period in your menstrual cycle. This is a brief guide to the different types of contraception. For more information go to a doctor or advice clinic (see page 102).

Oral contraceptives - the pill

These are excellent, but you must follow the instructions. They come in tablet form and you can get them from your doctor or advice clinic. Occasionally there are health scares about the pill. If you're worried see your doctor or advice clinic. Such scares are rare and having a baby is actually more dangerous – especially during adolescence when your body is not yet fully developed.

The 'morning after' pill

If you do have sex without using any contraceptives you can still stop a pregnancy – if you act fast. You can take the 'morning after' pill for up to 72 hours after sex to stop a pregnancy starting. You can get this pill from your doctor or family planning clinic.

Caps

These fit over the entrance to the vagina. Difficult to put in place and not always very reliable, you can get them from your doctor or advice clinic.

Coils

Coils (also called IUDs or intrauterine devices) fit into the uterus. They must be fitted by a doctor or nurse and are best for older women whose bodies have stopped growing. They are not as reliable as oral contraceptives.

Male condoms

The most readily available contraceptive, the condom is a soft rubbery sheath to put over an erect penis. This stops sperm entering the vagina and reaching an egg. Available at chemists, supermarkets, petrol stations and so on, condoms come in a range of sizes, colours and even shapes! As well as preventing pregnancy, condoms also protect against sexually transmitted diseases and the HIV virus.

Take care when you take off a condom. You must make sure that no sperm gets into the vagina – that could ruin all the trouble you've gone to. Condoms past their sell-by date are unsafe. And don't keep them in a warm place, like your pocket, for too long.

Female condoms

The female condom is like a soft pouch or rubbery bag made out of polyurethane which the woman inserts in her vagina. It doesn't fit tightly like the male condom, but lines the vagina to catch the sperm before they enter the womb. You may want to practise a few times to be sure you're using this condom properly. And don't forget that you might need to use both male and female condoms with a spermicide, a contraceptive foam, cream or jelly, to make extra sure that you/she doesn't become pregnant.

Contraceptive implants

Implants that release contraceptive substances into the body. They are only available from your doctor or advice clinic.

If your partner uses a coil or a cap, don't worry, you won't be able to feel it!

Deciding what contraception to use should be a joint decision. If your partner doesn't want to talk about it he/she probably isn't ready for a sexual relationship.

Contraceptive foams, creams and jellies

You can buy these from chemists and supermarkets. Follow the instructions, but most must be inserted into the vagina about 10 minutes before you have intercourse – and that's each time you are going to have sex. They are not that reliable and are best used with another form of contraception but using them makes for nice foreplay.

True or false?

Washing or showering immediately after sex gets rid of the sperm. **FALSE**.

A good method of contraception is for the man to withdraw his penis before ejaculating (coitus interruptus). **FALSE**. Why? An orgasm may take the man by surprise so he can't keep his promise to withdraw.

Sex standing up prevents pregnancy because sperm cannot swim uphill. **FALSE**.

Sources of advice

At some point you'll probably want advice from a proper 'expert' – someone who's had some training in the topics dealt with in this book. Your doctor is the best person, because he/she knows what's available locally. It can be awkward if you don't want your parents to know you've been, or why you've been. But doctors should respect a patient's (your) confidence and not pass anything on to your parents. Ask about this before saying anything – the chances are he/she'll have guessed why you've come anyway.

Family planning clinics are another source of help and advice (they're listed in the phone directory). And most large towns and cities have advice clinics especially for teenagers (see page 102). At these you will get advice that is impartial and confidential. It will also be non-judgemental: if you're in a mess they'll do their best to help you out of it – they won't say you shouldn't have got into it in the first place – but by then you'll know that anyway.

And don't forget the agony aunt pages in magazines!

They're always good reading!

The downsides of sex

Pregnancy

If you and your partner have decided to have sex, that's probably all you want – sex and not a baby. So, with a bit of luck, you'll have read – and talked about – the information on contraceptives on pages 78 and 79 and decided which to use.

If you haven't used contraceptives (and very occasionally even if you have), you may find you're pregnant. The signs are missing your period (but do remember that your periods may be erratic when you first start them) and possibly feeling sick, although not everyone who is pregnant does. If you're worried, especially if you've missed two periods, pregnancy testing kits are on sale in all large chemists and supermarkets. They're cheap, reliable and, best of all, are on the open shelves, so you don't even have to ask an assistant for one.

If you didn't use contraception and aren't pregnant you've had a lucky escape. If you are pregnant it's no good anyone saying 'don't panic', because you will. The first thing to do is to talk to someone who can give you advice and support – your parents are best. But if you can't talk to them, or want more help, there are some very good telephone helplines (see page 102) and the people you'll talk to will understand. You'll also need to tell to your partner you're pregnant, but it is you who will really have to decide what to do next.

Decisions, decisions

You have three choices:
- you can continue the pregnancy and keep the baby
- you can continue the pregnancy and give the baby for adoption
- you can end the pregnancy by having an abortion

This is such a major decision you'll need help and advice from your family, your doctor, your advice clinic and your partner, though he'll probably be in a panic too.

Abortion

An abortion, or termination of pregnancy, ends the pregnancy by removing the foetus. Miscarriages, in which a woman also loses her baby, are sometimes called 'spontaneous abortions', but they occur naturally and are fairly rare.

Abortions are usually only done in the first twelve weeks of pregnancy, when the foetus is tiny. They are safe if done by trained medical staff. In the UK before you can have an abortion two doctors must agree that it is the best thing for you. Some people believe it is wrong to have an abortion and end the life of the foetus, others think a woman should be able to choose for herself. Whatever they believe, most people agree that having to have an abortion is sad and that it is much better to think ahead and use contraception.

Sexually transmitted diseases (STDs)

Sex is usually a normal healthy part of life, but it can have dangers. Sexually transmitted diseases (STDs) are infections that both men and women can catch during sexual intercourse. Like coughs and colds these diseases are caused by tiny germs, such as bacteria and viruses. In the past these diseases were called 'venereal disease' or VD.

Chlamydia This is one of the most common STDs.

Gonorrhoea Another very common STD; it can be passed on to a baby when it is born. If you catch chlamydia or gonorrhoea you may find it stings when you pass water, and men may have a sticky liquid 'discharge' from the end of their penis. Women often have no symptoms and so don't realise they have the disease. This can be serious, because if a woman has the disease for a long time it may make it difficult for her to have babies. Both diseases can usually be completely cured with antibiotics, medicines to kill the bacteria, which your doctor will give you.

Herpes This is caused by a virus which spreads easily from skin to skin. There are two sorts: one causes blisters or 'cold sores' on the face, while the other causes blisters around the genitals. Herpes is a virus so antibiotics cannot cure it because they only work on bacteria. There are treatments, but the blisters usually go away on their own, although they may come back again.

Syphilis This is less common than other STDs but can be very serious. It is caused by bacteria and can be life threatening. It begins with a small, hard nodule (spot) near the genitals, but develops into an illness which affects the whole body. It can be treated with antibiotics.

Hepatitis B This virus is very contagious (catching) and is spread by sex and using dirty needles. If you have your ears or body pierced, or get a tattoo, you must make sure the needle is new, because if someone with hepatitis B used it before you, you are very likely to get the disease. There is no cure, but there is a vaccine to stop you getting it.

HIV/AIDS HIV is a virus which is passed on during sex or by sharing a needle (as in drug taking). Mothers with this virus can give it to their babies before they are born. Someone with the virus is said to be 'HIV positive' and is very likely to develop AIDS. This is a serious illness for which there is no cure and everyone who has got AIDS has died from it. Scientists all over the world are trying to find a treatment for the disease.

AIDS is always fatal, but it is ONLY transmitted through bodily fluids, such as blood and semen. You CANNOT get it from kissing or toilet seats.

Protect yourself

Although most of these STDs can be treated, it's much better not to get them in the first place. The best way to avoid them is by using a condom. Other forms of contraception, like the pill, only prevent pregnancy, they do not stop you getting STDs.

So use a condom every time you have sex and keep yourself safe. And don't let anyone tell you otherwise. Or, if they do, ignore them and whatever else you do, don't have sex with them.

Sexual abuse

Sexual abuse is sexual contact to which one person has not consented or, if they did consent, it was because they were forced to. Few victims of sexual abuse talk about it. They feel ashamed, upset, frightened, as if it was their fault. Their abuser may also threaten them with more harm if they tell anyone.

Rape

Rape is penetrative sex carried out without the consent of one of the people involved. Rape can cause lasting physical and mental harm to its victims. It is rarely an attempt to achieve sexual satisfaction. Instead it is usually an expression of anger, or of a desire to dominate or humiliate. The victims can be male or female. It is punishable by law. Rape is not just committed by strangers. It can be, and is, committed by anyone – a member of your family, by someone you know well, someone you know slightly. Indeed police statistics show that most rapists know their victims.

Date rape drugs

The most common of these is Rohypnol. It is tasteless, very powerful and usually put in the victim's drink without him/her knowing. Rohypnol causes unconsciousness and when you wake up you may not remember much about what you have done or where you have been. If you're going clubbing, say, especially if it's with people you don't know very well, don't leave your glass on the table unless it's empty, especially if the club's very crowded. If it isn't finished and you need to go to the toilet, take it with you. If you want to dance, finish the drink first. You can always go back to the dance floor, but there's no going back from rape.

If you are the victim of an attacker who has used this drug on you, you must go to the police – and whatever you do, don't have a bath or shower first.

Steps for staying safe

- Avoid dark and deserted places.
- Carry a torch and/or a personal alarm at night.
- Don't get into a car on your own with someone you don't know.
- Don't go to the home of someone you don't know unless you're in a group.
- Try to stay sober – especially if you're female.

Sexual abuse in the family

Sadly, sexual abuse, including rape, can happen within a family. It can be carried out by parents, step-parents or more distant relatives. If children are involved, they may be threatened and told that no one will believe them. They will also feel confused and guilty, as if it's their fault. It is never the child's fault. It is always the adult's fault. Such abuse causes immense harm to its victims, often making it very difficult for them to form good relationships with people when they grow up.

Paedophilia

Paedophilia, or child abuse, is sexual relations between a child and an older person. Like all forms of sexual abuse the damage it does to the victim is enormous. Occasionally there are reports in the media of children being abducted. Such cases are very, very rare – that is why they get so much media coverage.

Remember – sexual violence, rape and paedophilia are all illegal.

Important: If you suffer a sex attack do not wash or shower. Tell someone you trust and go at once to your doctor or nearest hospital. You may also need to go to the police.

Never, ever, fall for such statements as 'Don't tell anyone about this, it's our little secret' or 'Tell anyone and you'll regret it'. Find an adult you trust and do the opposite!

If anyone approaches you in an unpleasant way, walk, fast, in the opposite direction. If they continue after you, run. And if you've ever felt like screaming, now is your chance!

Sex-tras

Good, bad or...?

Swearing and bad language

Sex and bad language seem to go together like fish and chips. It's the same everywhere. Words for both male and female genitalia become terms of abuse. It's such a pity that sex, which can be so wonderful, is degraded in this way. And using these terms also degrades those who use them.

Yes, even the ancient Egyptians had swear words for sex. There's sexual graffiti in some of their wall paintings, but it's always in small private rooms. So perhaps using such terms in public was not a good idea then...

...and it certainly isn't now.

Erotica

Erotica is art or literature intended to arouse sexual feelings. So if you look at erotic pictures or read erotic books and feel aroused that's exactly what the artist or author intended you to feel! But you'll be surprised just how subtle erotica can be – there may not be a naked body in sight!

Oh really, surely you've seen better than that! Well, it's all individual anyway – what turns some people on might turn others off. You'll soon find out what you like and what you don't. And if you don't like the idea of looking at or reading erotica, it doesn't mean you're abnormal!

Oooh look at that... isn't he...?!

Top tip:

You can find erotic material at newsagents, cinemas and video rentals, but you'll be surprised just how much there is in libraries and even museums and art galleries. In those places it's called great art not erotica – but what's in a name?!

Love poems

Writing your partner a love poem can be very erotic – for you both. Try it!

Pornography

Pornography is also designed to arouse sexual desire but, unlike erotica, it does it in a crude and very explicit way. It always features nudes, and sexual activity is shown or described absolutely explicitly. Nothing is left to the imagination – sad really.

It is illegal to sell pornographic material of any sort to anyone under the age of 18.

Any form of visual pornography that involves children is illegal and anyone who has such material is prosecuted. The police can search the homes and remove computers belonging to suspects in such cases.

Prostitution

Prostitution is letting someone have sex with you in return for money. Both men and women can be prostitutes. A male prostitute is called a gigolo or rent boy.

Nicknamed the 'oldest profession', this is probably true because sex is something humans have always wanted. Prostitutes are at risk of violence and getting sexually transmitted diseases and the HIV virus. Although prostitution is legal in some countries, it is not in the UK. But, legal or not, it is still a hard and risky way to earn money.

Peeping Toms

Peeping Toms (also called voyeurs) secretly watch people petting, making love etc, while hiding behind bushes and generally lurking about. Sometimes they just watch, sometimes they also masturbate.

Peeping Toms are pathetic rather than dangerous, but meeting them is unpleasant. Ignore them, go home and tell your parents.

Flashers

Unlike Peeping Toms flashers get their kicks from being seen. They expose their genitals to unsuspecting members of the public.

If you meet a flasher move away quickly and tell an adult as soon as you can.

Orgies

Sex with more than two people involved – see picture!

Sexual myths – ancient

Narcissus

A youth who saw his image in a lake and fell in love with it, gradually wasting away until he died from unfulfilled desire for himself! Sad!

The gods turned his body into the flower now called after him. Today we say someone is narcissistic if he/she is very self-centred and obsessed with him/herself.

Oedipus

A rather careless (or shortsighted) young man who first killed his father, then married his mother and had four children by her – all without knowing that
   a) it was his father and
   b) it was his mother.

When they discovered they were mother and son (as well as husband and wife) they committed suicide.

Sodom and Gomorrah

Two cities described in the Old Testament of the Bible as being the pits in terms of their sinfulness. The cities, and everyone in them, came to a bad end! Today, sodomy means anal sex.

Sexual myths – modern

What's the point of old myths? There are plenty around today.

Here are a few.

Am I pregnant?

This must be about the most common question an agony aunt is asked. It reflects anxiety, but also ignorance – that's the myth bit.

> Dear Aunt Sybil
> Please help me! I am beside myself with worry. Our class went on a hiking trip last week. We walked for hours and I was so tired I almost fainted. When we reached the top I sat on a rock. A friend said that minutes before a boy called Jack from another class had sat on the rock and that I was probably pregnant – she knows I fancy him. I thought she was pulling my leg, but I think she must be right. I don't feel too well and my stomach seems to be getting bigger.
>
> Yours desperately,
>
> Jill

Dear Jill
You clearly haven't read any books about sex. If you had you would know that without sexual intercourse no one can get pregnant. Get yourself a copy of 'The Sex Files' and stop worrying!
Yours,
Aunt Sybil

Do you remember when you...

No I don't.

Coming nine times in a row

This is the dream of every male. As kids they dream about it, in their prime they work at it, and in their old age they talk about it. Their boyhood dream remains just that – a dream. This is Jason's story:

"When I first heard about the record I was ten. A boy in another class had done it in front of two witnesses. To help him he looked at a photo of a naked blonde lying on a rumpled bed. Since then I have tried to break this record. I have never succeeded. I shall be 60 tomorrow. What a failure!"

Aunty Gertie's comment: Jason would have been happier and enjoyed things far more if he'd had real sex with a real woman.

Aphrodisiacs

The desire for better sex is as old as sex itself. Aphrodisiacs are stimulants said to help fulfil that desire. Most are harmless fun – a good excuse to have another chocolate! But concentrating on your partner and your relationship with him/her is a **much** better way of having better sex!

No one in their right mind thinks alcohol or drugs increase sexual performance. The phrase 'drinker's droop' puts it in a nutshell!

Sex through history

In the bad old days parents decided who their children would marry. They said things like 'We're older and wiser than you', 'We know better than you', 'What do you know about it, you're far too young'. So marriages were arranged between the parents, and the bride and bridegroom often did not meet until the day of the wedding. Parents often made dreadful mistakes.

Today things have changed in many cultures and parents have no say in who their son/daughter marries. So now it's the children who may make the dreadful mistakes.

No sex before we're married – well, that's one approach, but it might not make for happy conversations and a relaxed relationship:

Remarks like those were made when girls wanted to make sure they were virgins when they married. In some societies it was (and still is) very important for a woman to be a virgin when she married. Her first experience of sexual intercourse was with her new husband on their wedding night. It didn't matter if the man was not a virgin too.

A virgin is described as being chaste – which is where the word 'chastity' comes from. But if a woman is married, being 'chaste' means not having sex with anyone except her husband. In the bad old days, when men could be away for years fighting wars, a wife was expected to be faithful to her husband and not have sex with anyone while he was away. What he did was quite another matter!

Although there are many old stories about men putting chastity belts on their wives before they left for the wars, not a single chastity belt has ever been discovered! Are they just another sexual myth?

What he got up to while he was away was another matter. But that's called having your cake and eating it!

Whether chastity belts are fact or fiction isn't important, what is important is being faithful to your partner. If you cheat on him/her why should he/she be faithful to you? And if you do cheat and start two-timing, why should a new partner trust you?

Just before we finish

With a bit of luck you've learnt something from these pages, or at least been reassured about something that's been worrying you. But, just to make sure you have:

a) really read the previous pages and
b) remembered what you've read, here's a test.

Proficiency tests

There are two tests:

1. Clothes on and clothes off

2. True or false

Scoring:

Ten points for a correct answer, five for a partly correct one and nothing if it's wrong. Add up all the points, multiply by two, subtract from the age of the oldest reader and divide by your grandfather's shoe size. Readers with the highest scores will receive a diploma.

DIPLOMA

Sex and Relationship Expert

1. Clothes on and clothes off

A very simple test. Paste a photocopy of this page onto some cardboard. Cut out the various drawing on the page. Then dress and undress the two figures as much as you like. If you do it with soft music playing and dimmed lights you can make believe you're doing it to...!

2 True or False

Now to test your knowledge of sexual matters. Put a T or an F after each statement according to whether you think the statement is true or false.

Erection – a rush of blood to the head

Prostitute/gigolo – someone who charges money for sex

Virgin – a girl or woman who has not had sexual intercourse

Impotence – a man's sexual potency

Bisexual – a man who only enjoys sex with women

Ejaculation – release of sperm by the female, so satisfying she wants to do it again

Heterosexual – someone sexually attracted to people of the opposite sex

Scrotum – plastic pouch containing the testes

Tip: You will have to hold the page up to a mirror to reveal the answers.

Scrotum – a pouch of skin containing the testes

Heterosexual – someone sexually attracted to people of the opposite sex

Ejaculation – release of sperm by the male, so satisfying he wants to do it again

Bisexual – someone sexually attracted to people of both sexes

Impotence – a man's lack of sexual potency

Virgin – a girl or woman who has not had sexual intercourse

Prostitute/gigolo – someone who charges money for sex

Erection – a surge of blood to the penis

Goodbye, enjoy your life – and your sexual life. Think of it like a rose, for a rose can be beautiful and give joy and pleasure. But if you're not careful it can cause pain too. As always, it's your choice.

We're on your side. Don't let yourself be lied to, cheated on or used, but don't do it to others either. Have fun, take care – and good luck!

USEFUL CONTACTS

British Pregnancy Advisory Service
(BPAS)
Austy Manor
Wootten Wawen
Solihull B95 6BX
Tel: 01564 793225
Actionline (appointments):
  08457 30 40 30
website: www.bpas.org
Information and treatment for
unplanned pregnancy.

Childline
Freepost 1111
London N1 0BR
Tel: 0800 1111
website: www.childline.org.uk
A free 24-hour helpline offering advice
and help for children in trouble or
danger.

fpa (formerly know as the Family
Planning Association)
2–12 Pentonville Road
London N1 9FP
Tel: 0845 310 1334
website: www.fpa.org.uk
Information and advice on
contraception, sexual health and
abortion.

Rape Crisis Federation
Unit 7, Provident Works
Newdigate Street
Nottingham NG7 4FD
Tel: 0115 900 3560
Fax: 0115 900 3562
website: www.rapecrisis.co.uk
Support and advice for anyone who has
been raped or sexually abused.

Samaritans
PO Box 90 90
Stirling
FK8 2SA
Tel: 08457 90 90 90 (UK)
Tel: 1850 60 90 90 (Republic of
Ireland)
website: www.samaritans.org.uk
Confidential support for anyone feeling
anxious, depressed or suicidal.

**Sexual Health and National AIDS
Helpline**
Tel: 0800 567 123
A 24-hour confidential service offering
advice on all aspects of sexual health,
HIV and AIDS.

Index

periods (*see* menstruation)
petting 59
pornography 9, 48-49, 91
pregnancy 36, 37, 59, 64, 67, 69, 74-75,
   78-79, 82, 95
premature ejaculation 70
progesterone 10
prostitution 91
puberty 10, 15, 28, 32, 36, 54

R

rape 85
relationships 24, 53, 54, 55, 56

S

sanitary towels 36, 37
school 16, 20-21
scrotum 40
sex education 9, 21
sexual abuse 85, 86
sexual fantasies 49, 50
sexual intercourse 61-62, 63-64, 83
sexually transmitted diseases (STDs) 59,
   64, 79, 83-84, 91
   chlamydia 83
   gonorrhoea 83
   hepatitis B 84
   herpes 83
   HIV/AIDS 79, 84, 91
   syphilis 84
shyness 23, 24, 56
sperm 10, 36, 40, 51, 52, 64
spots (*see* acne)

T

tampons 36, 37
testicles 40
testosterone 10

U

uterus 36, 40, 64, 79

V

vagina 37, 39, 40, 61, 62, 68, 70, 79
virginity 59, 68, 97
voice 32

W

websites 9, 102
weight 30
wet dreams 52
womb (*see* uterus)